CIRUELO

'The quest for beauty is the only protest that is worthwhile.'

'Beauty is not something that belongs only to certain classes of people or things or jobs. On the contrary, every profession, every person or every thing has an inner beauty which is necessary to discover.'

Text by NIGEL SUCKLING

Paper Tiger

Paper Tiger Books
An imprint of Dragon's World Ltd
Limpsfield
Surrey RH8 0DY
Great Britain

First published 1990
Reprinted 1991

British Library Cataloguing in Publication Data
Cabral, Ciruelo
    Ciruelo.
    1. Argentinian illustrations. Cabral, Ciruelo
    I. Title II. Suckling, Nigel
    741.982

ISBN 1-85028-130-0 (*Hardback*)
ISBN 1-85028-134-3 (*Limpback*)

Editor Michael Downey
Designer Bob Gordon
Art Director Dave Allen
Editorial Director Pippa Rubinstein

Typeset by Dragon's World Ltd
Printed in Spain

CONTENTS

INTRODUCTION

Ciruelo Cabral was born in Buenos Aires and lived in Argentina until 1987 when he moved with little more than his wife, airbrush and guitar to Spain.

Ciruelo means literally 'plum tree' and is a nickname he acquired at school for reasons which he never quite grasped and which will now probably remain forever obscure. It was not a name he particularly liked but somehow it stuck and eventually took over. When he began using it to sign pictures, Ciruelo discovered that the name does in fact have some practical value as once people have grasped it they rarely forget it. English speakers usually have trouble with the pronunciation at first but only because they try to run the middle letters together to make a word of three syllables instead of four, which is how it should be. All one need do to obtain a fair approximation of the Spanish sound is begin with a soft 'c' and use the most common pronunciation for each following letter in turn.

The only formal art training Ciruelo (see, it is not so hard to say after all?) received was at school between the ages of thirteen and eighteen. One of the specialities taught was advertising, which proved useful later when it came to finding work. Another was craftsmanship, including bookbinding which in many ways had a greater impact because it introduced him to the technique of marbling which, as we shall see later, has been a constant fount of inspiration for Ciruelo besides accounting for the rich textures in many of his pictures.

Was he a born illustrator, scribbling away on every available scrap of paper since before he could walk? Well, partly yes, partly no. Drawing has always been a passion but not the only one. Equally important in his youth were sport and music and if either had beckoned him more seductively on leaving school it is quite possible that his artistic flair would have dwindled to little more than a hobby.

With hindsight Ciruelo is relieved the option of sport was not open to him, as might well have happened if he had lived, for example, in the United States. It is after all a young person's field and however successful you are the question soon arises of what to do with the rest of your life. Fortunately the option was never a serious one because rugby, his great love, is an amateur sport in Argentina and in athletics, his second string, sponsors were and probably still are pretty thin on the ground.

Music remains a serious temptation though. Ciruelo played in several bands as a teenager and if tomorrow he were to be offered a serious chance of swapping his airbrush for a guitar he cannot say which he would choose. What kind of music does he like? A wide range – 1970s 'symphonic' rock music in the vein of

The Crystal Shard (1990)

6

Yes and Genesis, jazz, salsa, and classical. Favoured classical composers are J. S. Bach, Handel, Debussy, and Ravel. Current non-classical favourites include Night Noise and the Pat Metheny Group, but he listens to almost any music when working.

However (to return to our story), when Ciruelo left school, art seemed the only one of his talents with any immediate future. Art college was considered briefly, but what was really needed was a job so he joined an advertising agency as a general dogs-body and slave. A year later he graduated to being an illustrator and a year later still he went freelance, which he has remained ever since.

Working at the agency was a great education. Shortage of money as a teenager meant that most of his pictures up to then had been done in pencil and ballpoint pen. At the agency he suddenly had access to an airbrush, acrylics and other media with which he could experiment in his free time. An example of this can be seen on page 74. Also he learned the necessary discipline for an illustrator – that of working with an art director. Perhaps most useful of all, he found piles of books of great illustrations from around the world which gave him an idea of what he was competing against.

The examples of his early work shown in this book give an idea of how rapidly Ciruelo's skill matured at this time, even after making allowances for their retouching and improvement. One consequence of this after he began freelancing and dealing with clients, mostly by post and telephone, was that they tended to assume from the strength and confidence of his work that he was much older than he was. When he first met his future wife Daniela at the advertising agency where she worked she assumed he was just Ciruelo Cabral's messenger.

The same mistake is still often made today but this is only partly due to his natural precocity. Buenos Aires is a forcing ground for the development of any illustrator, apparently. There is no shortage of work but the pay is low and the competition fierce. Add to this Argentina's economic problems and an illustrator has to work about twenty hours a day just to survive.

As a training this was not a bad thing but as a way of life it had its drawbacks. Much of the work, for example, was not very satisfying, so Ciruelo was forced to use the little spare time he had to test out his own ideas. Eventually the pressures rose to the point where he decided to follow the example of several other Argentine illustrators and move to Europe. A two month visit assured him of there being enough work in Spain. So without more ado he packed his bags and came to Barcelona.

Was it not a wrench, suddenly uprooting himself from home and family and starting a new life thousands of miles away? Of course, but he feels it was a necessary decision and has yet to find any reason to regret it.

Genesis (1990)
This is a free illustration done purely for its own sake and at about a metre tall is twice the size of most of Ciruelo's pictures. The idea sprang from an old piece of marbling discovered on a return visit to Argentina and took about a week to complete. He would like to have spent at least twice as long on it but the time for such free works has to be stolen from his professional schedule. The underlying theme is a common one in Ciruelo's free work – the vindication of nature against man. Here we see the meeting in a kiss of two opposite forces of nature, air and water represented by fish and eagle, with man nowhere at all in the picture.

FANTASY

As a child Ciruelo was always interested in drawing but what really fired his imagination at the age of fifteen was the discovery of Roger Dean's work. Shock is the word he uses to describe his reaction. Suddenly he realized the kind of artwork he really wanted to do. Other heroes soon followed like Frank Frazetta, a really important influence, and Brian Froud. Then at the age of nineteen he discovered two Argentine illustrators who have remained lasting influences – Carlos Nine, who is rated as the best in the world, and Oscar Chichoni.

Oscar Chichoni, now resident in Italy, he admires for having developed a really personal style within the discipline of commercial illustration. This is at least partly due to his habit of illustrating his own ideas in his spare time and then looking for outlets through which to publish them, a less common habit among illustrators than one might imagine. It is a practice Ciruelo follows and is responsible for many of his strongest pictures, quite apart from the feedback effect it has on his commissioned work. These 'free works', as they are described, point the way to what we might expect from Ciruelo in the future, given the necessary freedom, but he is quick to point out that he does not feel he has found his truly personal style yet, which is why he is always experimenting with different techniques and fresh approaches.

Other influences include Norman Rockwell, Maxfield Parish, Katsu Yoshida (admired for his wide range of styles), and Masao Saito, considered by many to be the greatest exponent of hyperealism. That is to say, paintings whose subjects seem even more real than they are, or at least as they appear in photographs. Ciruelo's only reservation about Saito's work is that it is confined to subjects which could just as easily be photographed instead of using the technique to create new possibilities. However, that is not necessarily a criticism, only a statement of Ciruelo's own ambition.

His aunt Cecilia is the only member of his family Ciruelo can remember having any artistic influence on him because she was studying art while he was at an impressionable age (though she did not pursue it later). But in Spain he has found a new family of fellow Argentine exiles who are also illustrators. Two of an older generation are Juan Gimenez and Horacio Altuna who are a constant source of encouragement and advice. Then there is his childhood friend Gusti with whom he cycles in the hills and rates as almost a twin brother, even down to their being born within a week of each other.

Azure Bonds (1989)
Cover for a book in the *Forgotten Realms* series. Ciruelo would really have preferred to do a full-length portrait of this heroine but bowed to the publisher's wishes and is in fact quite pleased with the result. For the background he used a new technique of razor-scraping a plain coloured surface to get highlights, then adding shadows.

Gusti helped blaze the trail to Spain by moving there a year earlier than Ciruelo, choosing the small town of Sitges where they all now live. The attraction of Sitges is that not only is it a pretty town on the Mediterranean coast backed by mountains and with a wonderful view of the sunset, but it is only forty kilometres from Barcelona. Thus there is plenty of work for artists and illustrators who form a sizeable part of the population.

The Cabral home is a fourth floor flat overlooking the town and sea. It is also the studio where they both work, Daniela also being an illustrator who helps with the masking and airbrushing of Ciruelo's work. The contrast with Buenos Aires, where no illustrator dares live away from the capital for fear of losing work, is so delightful that the only reason they can think of for moving is the offer of irresistible work elsewhere. They still want to see as much as possible of the world but, ideally, with Sitges remaining their base. Countries they particularly wish to visit are Peru, Mexico, Egypt, and Turkey, whose surrealistic landscapes and architecture remind Ciruelo of Roger Dean fantasies.

Is the lot of a professional illustrator in Catalonia complete heaven then, after the rigours of Argentina? Well no, not quite, apparently. The pressures which drove Ciruelo to emigrate have lessened but not vanished altogether. He enjoys more of his work now but still not all of it, he has more time for free work but still not enough, and the fantasy illustration which he loves still does not pay a great deal. So, life is not perfect but it is a great improvement and the future looks bright. Any doubts about the wisdom of embarking on a new life in a strange continent are squashed by occasional telephone conversations with his mentor Carlos Nine who claims that the pressures at home are easing but still works at a horrendous pace by Spanish standards.

Meanwhile in Spain Ciruelo is reaping the benefit of his time on the Buenos Aires treadmill and is constantly surprised by meeting European contemporaries who seem only just deciding what to do with their lives, let alone building up a body of work with which to stake their place in the world. What direction would Ciruelo like his fantasy work to take in the future? Well, he says, for an illustrator it is not easy to plan ahead because so much depends on the luck of the commissions that come your way. But, apart from finding more time for his own free work, he would love to get involved in film costume design, about which he is a firm believer in the doctrine that even the wildest costumes should also be practical.

Also he would like to work on a larger scale and spend at least twice as long on each picture, for which he believes it will be necessary to reach a wider international audience, of which there are some encouraging signs. France and the United States are particularly tempting because fantasy publishers there have larger budgets for their cover art.

Spellfire (1989)
One of several covers for a series of books by various authors published under the collective label *Forgotten Realms*, for which Ciruelo also provided the Spanish logo (see page 117).

Black Wizards (1989)
Also for the *Forgotten Realms* series. Usually these covers are commissioned while translation is still under way so the illustration has to be based on a synopsis or suggestions from the publisher. Sometimes all they want is a slight modification of the original English-language cover, but in this case Ciruelo was given almost a free hand with the character and, as usual, the strength of the result is in direct proportion to this freedom.

Darkwell (1989)
Book cover for the *Forgotten Realms* series.

Captain Beto from Haedo (early work)
An early work executed on a much larger scale than usual. The model is a famous
Argentine performer whose music and poetry Ciruelo grew up with. The song
illustrated here is about an Argentine cosmonaut and to emphasize his nationality.

ABOVE **Weasel's Luck** (1989)

Darkwalker on Moonshae (1989)
In this case the overall composition was decided by the publishers so originality was confined to the detail work. A nice touch is that the female is playing a more active part in her defence than is common in fantasy.

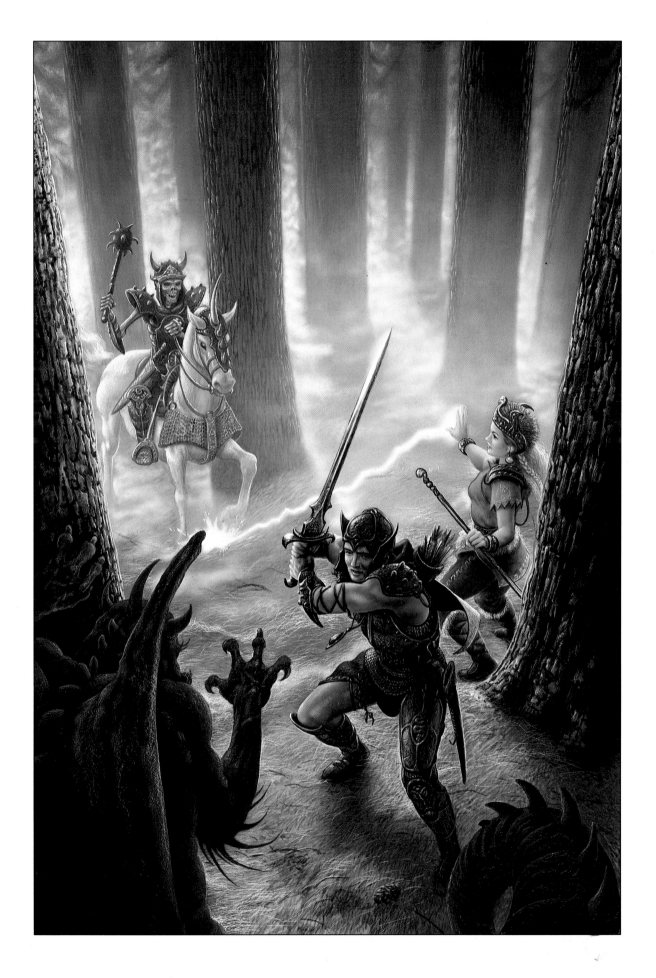

Jabato (1989)
The cover of a computer game starring
a famous Spanish comic book
character.

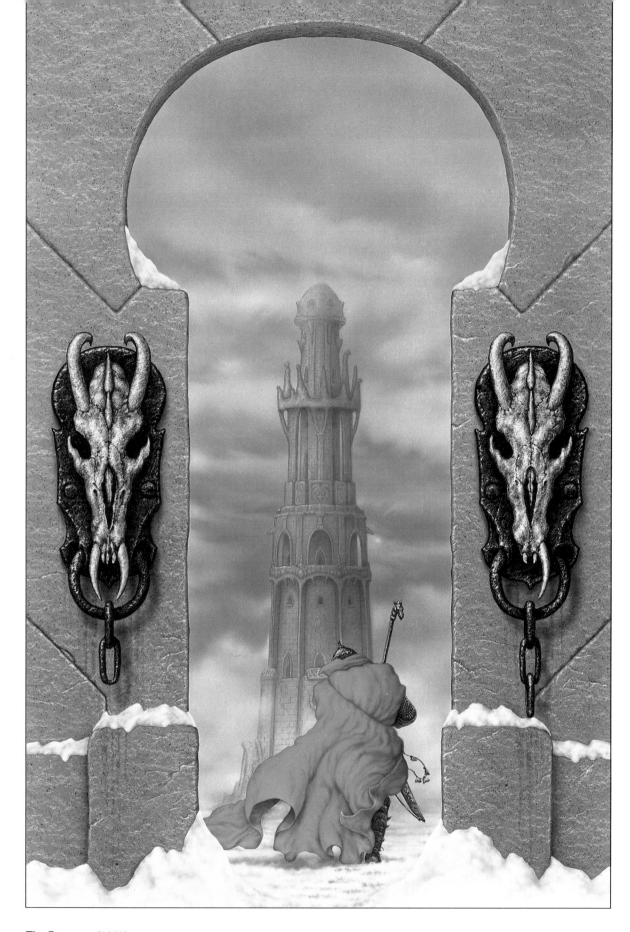

The Dungeon (1989)

Cover illustration for a Philip José Farmer novel. The basic idea of a tower seen through a gateway was suggested by the publishers, along with the request for a single small character in the foreground, but otherwise Ciruelo was given a more or less free hand. In this case having a diminished character seen from behind is very effective, and the picture has caught the attention of some New York publishers who are interested in commissioning more of such work, but usually Ciruelo would prefer to make his characters bolder to give more scope for portraiture.

Sueñero (early work)
An early work produced at the age of nineteen for a magazine cover in Argentina. As with other early works of which Ciruelo is fond, it has been retouched many times to bring it up to the technical standard of his current work. The delightfully lecherous abductor is the creation of Enrique Breccia, a famous Argentine comic artist and the scene is a fleshed-out excerpt from one of his stories.

RIGHT **Husmeante** (early work)
Another cover for the same Argentine magazine. The main character was originally created by the comic artist Mandrafina.

The Prophet of Akhran (1990)

The Will of the Wandered (1989)

The Paladin of the Night (1989)
With the two pictures opposite, this was
a set of cover illustrations for a trilogy
by Margaret Weis and Tracy Hickman,
for who Ciruelo has done much work.

OVERLEAF **Leisure Odyssey** (early work)
An early work for *Playboy* magazine in Argentina, illustrating an article
about what life would be like with every possible amenity or diversion
laid on. One possible conclusion can almost be read in a thought bubble
over the main character's head – extreme boredom. Ciruelo designed
everything in the picture from scratch to fit his imagined scenario. For
example, the serving robot on the right he imagined as a first-generation
model and so gave it an ape-like appearance. Behind it is a mobile
camera which can be sent wherever the owner chooses, and so on.

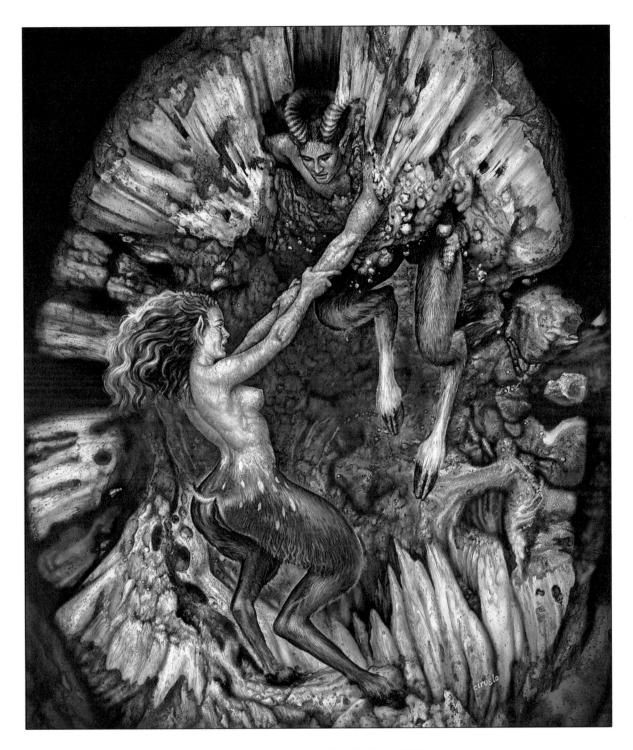

LEFT The Kidnapping (1985)
This is one of several illustrations for Ciruelo's 'Magma'
project described in the next chapter. Briefly, the tale is about
various races living in the centre of the world; mostly in
harmony but, as we see here, not always. The rich texture of
the background comes from starting with a marbled surface.

The Birthing (1985)
In the underground world of Magma the creatures and
people are born directly from the rock, so here in this
egg-shaped hollow we see one being helped into the world.

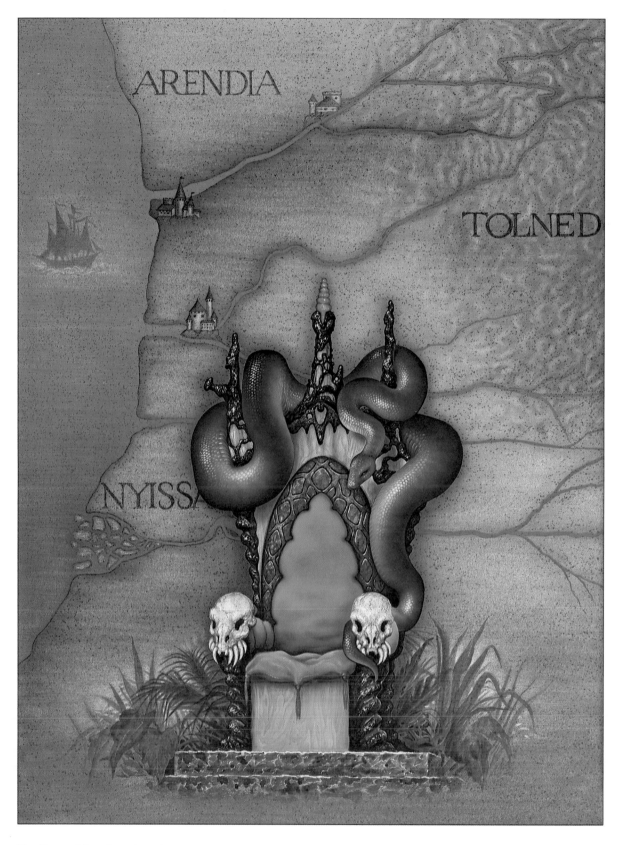

The Pawn of Prophecy (1989)
Cover for one of the *Belgariad* series of novels by David Eddings.

RIGHT **Queen of Sorcery** (1989)
Belgariad cover.

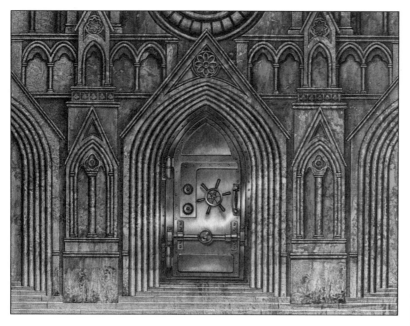

The Church's Treasure (early work)
An early work done at the age of twenty for a *Playboy* article about the
wealth of the church. The building's texture was again achieved by
working on a marbled surface.

Pollution (1989)
Illustration for an article in Spanish
Playboy.

Forging the Darksword (1988)

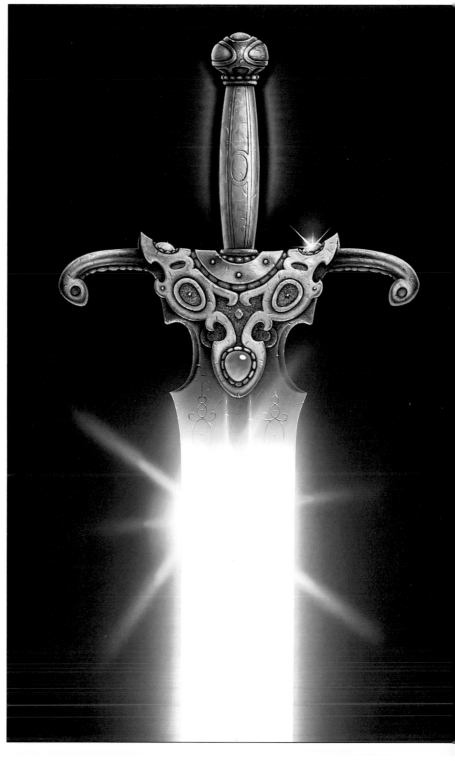

Triumph of the Darksword (1988)

RIGHT **Doom of the Darksword** (1988)
With the two illustrations above, this
comprises a set of covers for another
trilogy by Margaret Weis and Tracy
Hickman entitled *The Sword of Joram*.

LEFT Dragon Skull (1989)
A free work to investigate a new technique in which an airbrushed
background is scraped to get highlights, and shadows then added. The
original is much smaller than Ciruelo's usual size of about 50 x 40 cm.

Heroes Stormblade (1989)
Book cover.

WOMEN

Ciruelo would love to be asked to paint women more often than he is now, as is reflected in the fact that most of the pictures in this section are free work. The main problem is that in Spain recently there has been a fashion for book covers without human figures, or on such a small scale that no real portraiture is possible. Sometimes this works well but mostly Ciruelo is impatient for the fashion to change. In his illustrations for *Playboy* the chance does not often arise because the articles he is given are frequently on news topics. So, these pictures were mostly painted for love not money. His wife Daniela is his model when not working from photographs.

The first set of pictures rely heavily on marbling so this is perhaps an appropriate place to expand on the subject. As mentioned earlier, Ciruelo first discovered the technique while learning bookbinding at school. It was taught only as a means of producing colourful endpapers for hand-bound books but Ciruelo immediately saw a wealth of other possibilities in the swirling, vivid patterns – pictures begging to be dragged from chaos into the light of the ordered world. In short, he fell in love with marbling and has used it as a source of ideas ever since.

The technique is simple enough to explain. Basically one just sprinkles a more or less random mixture of oil, water and ink onto one piece of paper and blot it with another. Describing what Ciruelo sees in the result is harder.

'For me' he says, 'marbling is like a cross-section of the space–time continuum, like a laser cutting a slice through formless smoke and revealing the beautiful swirling patterns of its motion. The movement of smoke shown by the laser is just like the mixing of oil, water and ink in marbling. Or to put it another way, at every moment we are surrounded by invisible waves, radio waves, television waves, all kinds of waves on different frequencies. Marbling is a way of capturing these waves as if on a photograph, like the laser in a smoky room.' It is not just a random mechanical process, in other words, but a window onto some hidden reality.

About the painting of women in general, and these marbled women in particular, he says: 'When I do illustrations of women's bodies I generally base myself on photographs but I never follow them faithfully. Some details are erased and some exaggerated a little. Depending on the movement or position, some lines or wrinkles that go unnoticed in the photograph would stand out badly in the illustration. In the same way, adding them to another part of the body heightens the erotic effect. It all depends on the observation angle of the model and the part of the body I am drawing.

Marbled Woman (1986)
Ciruelo's first experiment with adding marbled textures to human skin, done at the age of about twenty. The figure emerged from many preparatory sketches, finally being traced onto the marbled paper and having the shadows and background added by airbrush.

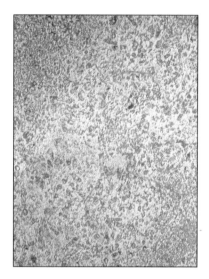

Here a marbled surface has been prepared for an experiment in which the same texture is to be given to both foreground and background. Usually marbling is achieved by mixing water, ink and oil on the surface but here an airbrush was used with free masking.

'I especially like to add strange textures to the skin, like marble or stone, because in this way I am adding an aesthetic attraction that enhances the feminine forms. So, often I start to work the figure on a blotted ink background. I shape the body like a sculptor, airbrushing in the shadows and depths, then with a hand brush introduce the highlights and exalting the texture of the stone. Essentially what I aim for is to give these figures the appearance of sculptures while remaining attractive as women.'

Several of these marbled women appeared in a feature on Ciruelo's work in the Spanish magazine *New Look* in 1989. They are also illustrations for a private project on which he works intermittently called 'Magma', a kind of fairytale which encapsulates everything he holds dear.

The basic postulate of the story is the existence at the centre of the earth of many different cultures and races, some of whom could almost be human apart from the curious rocky texture of their skins. This derives from the fact that, like all the other subterranean races, they are in fact earth-born creatures who spring fully grown from a magical and living pool of magma deep underground. Hence the story's title.

Through a kind of telepathy these people are well aware of

Now the image is traced on and shaded by airbrush.

Marbled Model (1988)
The final image. The addition of the robot hands and clapperboard was prompted by an international festival of fantastic movies in Ciruelo's home town of Sitges. When time permits he would like to expand the scene to show the model on a film set surrounded by cameras, film crew, director and so on.

Gioconda (1986)
An early work executed on a larger scale than usual and part of a set
produced with the aim of interesting galleries in his work. Ciruelo
discovered, however, as many others have done, that the fine art
world looks down its nose at anything which smacks of 'illustration'.
Since then he has made a point of describing himself as an
illustrator rather than an artist.

RIGHT **Marbled Legs** (1988)

events on the earth's surface but they keep their own existence secret because of the human race's alienation from nature, which they see as the cause of most of our wars and disasters.

So, from a safe distance they keep an eye on human affairs and occasionally communicate in a veiled way with some individuals who seem more enlightened than the rest. Like a certain Leonardo da Vinci, for example, whom they inspired with the image of one of their own great works of art. However, they cannot keep their distance entirely because every 2000 years or so the pool of magma to which they owe their existence needs a drop of the sun in order to survive. In other words, it needs direct contact with something or someone from the civilization of the sun on the surface.

Into the scene comes Ciruelo's hero, a passionate sculptor called Hervé. Through his art and possibly with some prompting from below he begins to suspect the existence of the underground people. His search for evidence leads to a pyramid where suddenly the ground opens up and swallows him. Whether this is in reality or a vision is not quite clear but either way he arrives in the subterranean world where he is given a number of tasks to fulfil before he can leave.

In the course of the following adventures he falls in love, meets some very strange people, and learns several lessons

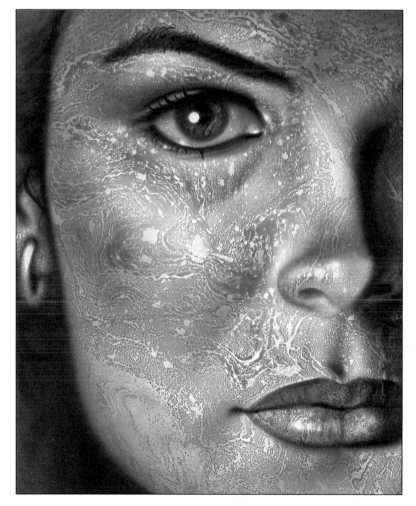

Marbled Face (1986)

RIGHT **France** (1989)
Illustration for a Spanish *Playboy* article achieved mostly by scraping a painted surface and afterwards shading the main figure.

Marbled Shower I (1988)
This picture and the following one were the result of an experiment in textures. For this second version Ciruelo worked on a photograph of the original, a slightly tricky process because of the peculiar surface of photographic paper. Trickier still was marbling the woman's skin because the pattern had to fit closely a pre-determined area, a reverse of the usual procedure.

RIGHT **Marbled Shower II** (1988)
At the end of the Magma story the hero returns to the surface with evidence to prove the existence of the underground people – a photograph which clearly shows the curious rocky nature of their flesh. However, when he gets home he finds the picture has mysteriously changed into this one which proves nothing more than that some people look more attractive when taking a shower than others.

about civilization which could usefully be applied to the war-torn world from which he comes (the setting is the twenty-first century after World War Three), but more than this it would probably be unsporting to say.

In a way Ciruelo believes the story to be true, with only the reservation whether Hervé's adventures happen within the crust of our concrete world or on another plane of existence hidden from but accessible to human consciousness, given the right conditions. What he definitely believes is that the earth has an intelligent soul and is both wiser and more powerful than the human race, that we only exist on sufferance and the day we push our luck too far the earth will wipe us out and begin some more rewarding experiment.

For this reason he does not believe it possible for mankind to destroy the earth through either ecological disaster or nuclear war. Conversely, he believes that if one respects and loves the earth, it will do the same in return. In his own case, love for nature is so ingrained in Ciruelo that no conscious virtue is involved. He just simply cannot understand, for example, someone who tosses an empty drink can away over their shoulder when out in the country.

The Magma story came close to being taken up by a publisher recently but was shelved in favour of a book about dragons which Ciruelo is to illustrate. However, we have probably not heard the last of it.

In Ciruelo's free work women usually symbolize the side of human nature closest to instinct and the rest of the natural world. He is aware that this could be interpreted as a rather male chauvinist view but really it is almost the opposite. To him communion with nature is the most important thing in life, not just for artists and illustrators, but for people in any walk of life.

This has always been his view despite growing up and living most of his life in Buenos Aires where most natural greenery has been resolutely banished beyond the city limits. By way of compensation both his grandfathers had ranches some 2000 kilometres north of the capital on the edge of almost Amazonian jungle where he and his brother Jorge used to spend their summers. There Ciruelo fell in love with nature and would spend many hours sitting on a rock or in a tree, trying almost to become that very thing.

Also, when roaming the woods and jungles he had a natural respect for everything he found – plants, trees and animals alike, he tried not to harm them. Which, when you think about it, is quite strange because the almost universal instinct of small boys is to occasionally smash and burn things and throw rocks at any wild animals rash enough to come within range. This attitude of respect has persisted and crystallized into a general belief that to earn respect one must first be ready to give it.

Years later Ciruelo found many of his childhood intuitions reflected and amplified in the writings of Carlos Castaneda (*The Teachings of Don Juan*, etc.). Also in many other, mostly oriental, philosophies which led him to the conclusion that the mystical branches of all religions have the same essential roots, but for him Castaneda expresses these ideas most clearly. In particular the idea that while humans usually stick to one plane of consciousness there are many others open to us. One of which is the plane on which we can communicate directly with nature, which lies somewhere along the way to the ultimate level where our individual consciousness merges with that of the whole of creation. Or, to put it in Ciruelo's own terms, when we realize that we are just one ripple in the vast piece of marbling which is the unfolding universe.

He does not believe he is at all unique in having such insights, or glimpses of insights, as a child. His wife Daniela agrees, saying: 'For instance, when a child says she has been speaking with the wind her parents don't believe it. But often she has.' Perhaps the strangeness is just that he did not repudiate or forget them as he grew older.

Interaction (1989)
One of the culture shocks Ciruelo felt on arrival in Spain came from the Roman ruins he found – ancient crumbling arches with trees forcing their way through the cracks, a vivid example of nature finally reconquering the proudest human artifacts. That was the starting point for this picture. The female is an ecologist in love with nature, represented of course by the tree that is slowly recapturing its rightful space usurped by the arch. At the same time the tree is wounded by the piping of technology.

Naked Back (1989)
Another recent free work in which new forms were being looked for. Introducing marginally abstract elements into an otherwise natural setting was again something Ciruelo had never tried before.

RIGHT **Erotic Nightmares** (1989)
A recent free work which was again an experiment in contrasting textures – cold, gritty and rusting metal against warm, vibrant flesh, symbolizing the decadence of technology beside the natural primitive beauty of nature. Ciruelo is contemplating a series of pictures in this vein set in a kind of post-holocaust era. The title springs from Ciruelo's realization one day that he had never used the colour green in pictures for more than foliage and minor details, so for him it is almost the main feature of the work.

PREVIOUS PAGE **Devil Girl** (1990)
Short story illustration for *Playboy.*

India (1987)
For a year after his move to Spain
Ciruelo produced video covers like this
for mainly Norwegian and Swiss clients
through an agency.

RIGHT **Strange New Hairdo** (1986)
Free work starting from a marbled
background.

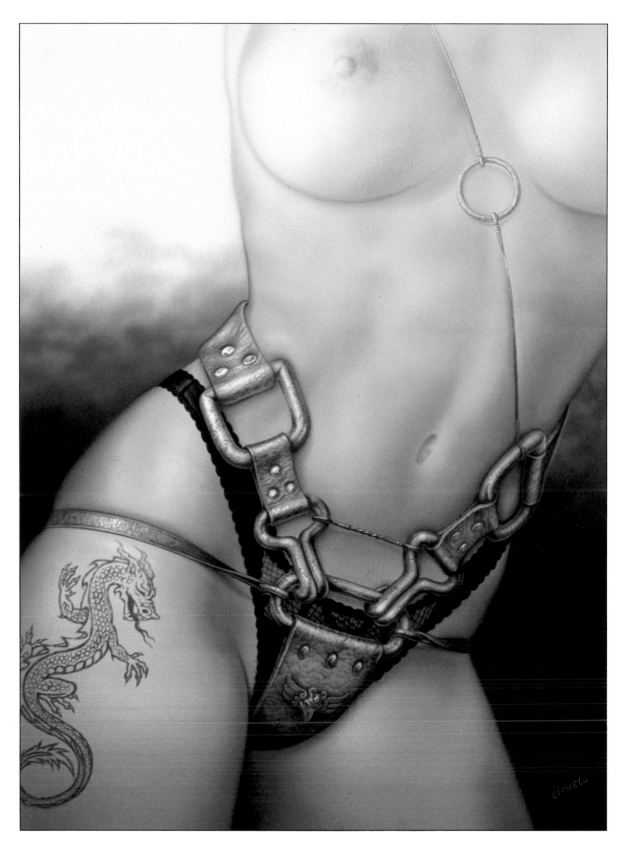

Tattoo (1987)

RIGHT **Lovers' Quarrel** (1989)
An exercise in hyperealism which also argues the case that
the best use of this technique is to make the impossible real.

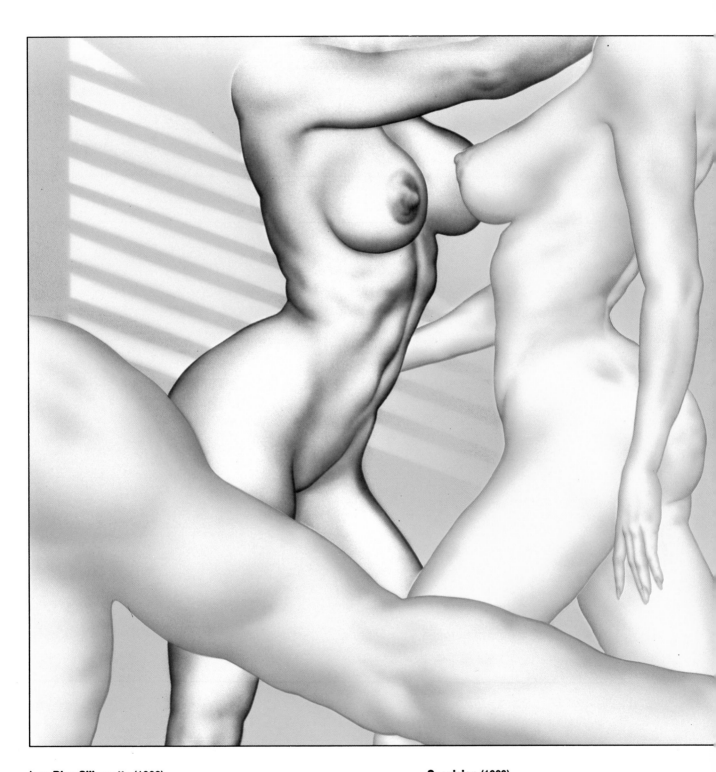

LEFT **Blue Silhouette** (1988)   **Suspicion** (1989)

LEFT **Playboy, I love you** (1986)

Champagne (1989)
One of a set of six illustrations Ciruelo completed in as many days.
His condition at the end can easily be imagined but it seemed
worthwhile because the fee paid for a trip back to Argentina.

Nudes in pastel (1989)
A series of sketches prompted by
Ciruelo's admiration of Katsu Yoshida
who continually experiments with style
and is a great believer in constant
drawing, a habit which illustrators can,
strangely enough, lose.

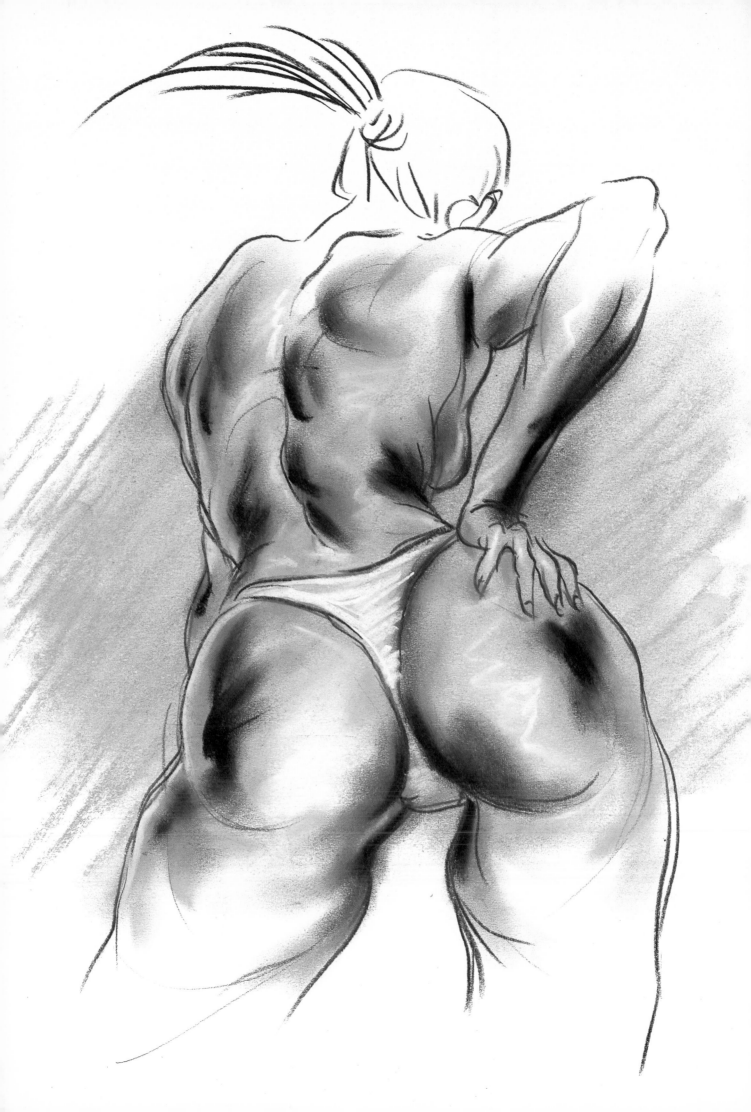

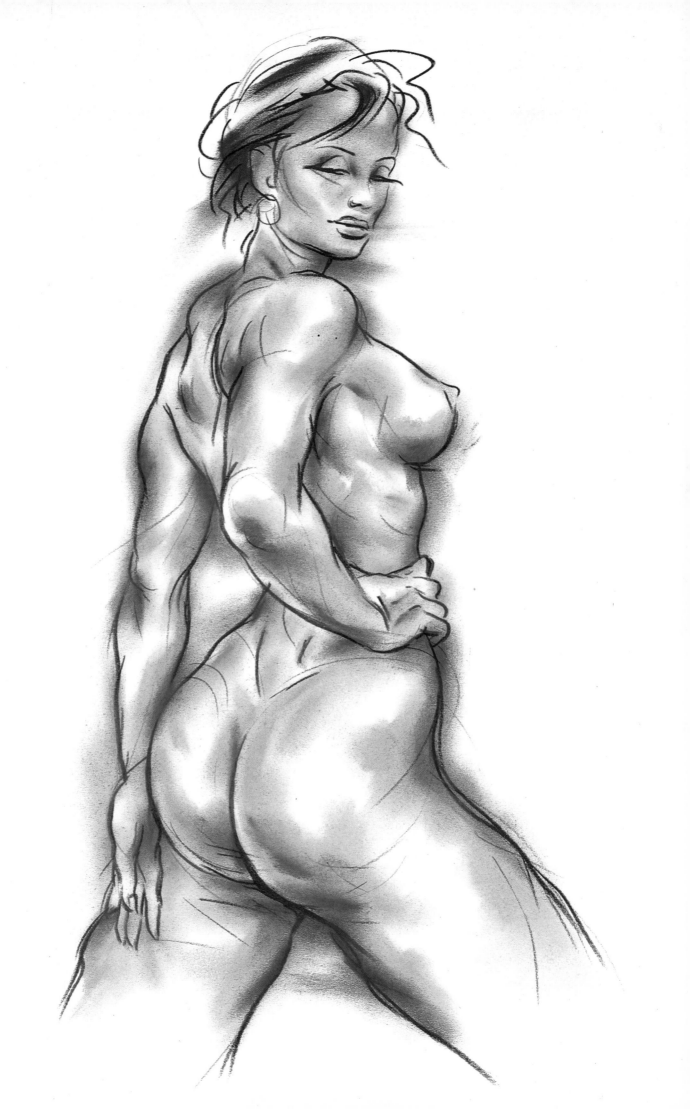

Ice Cream (1986
Illustration for *Playboy* article in
Argentina

CONCEPTS

Other illustrators have sometimes suggested that Ciruelo has too many different styles and should specialize more. But he feels that until he finds a truly personal style with which he is completely happy the way forward is to try as many others as present themselves, even if they appear to be pulling in different directions as, for example, in the often simultaneous attraction he feels towards Saito-type hyperrealism and the watercolours of Brian Froud and Alan Lee.

One benefit of this is that different styles can occasionally be brought together to produce new and often startling effects which in a way are the hallmark of Ciruelo's best pictures and probably represent the personal style he is looking for and has, in fact, already found without quite realizing it. As with many illustrators, getting his hands on an airbrush was a great liberation, a quantum leap, although he rarely uses it for the whole of a picture.

Unlike most airbrush artists he uses masking film (thin plastic film laid over the painting and carefully cut out with a scalpel around the area to be painted next) as little as possible. Instead he prefers to use a free airbrush with perhaps some hand-held, moveable masking. This is not just a personal preference, but it springs from the fact that in Argentina masking film was virtually unobtainable – he has had years of practise in doing without.

The problem with art materials was not just that most of them had to be imported and so were expensive, but that most of the imports used to come from England and with the trade embargo following the Falklands–Malvinas conflict the supply dried up almost completely. In airbrushing this led to often hilarious (looking back on it) improvisations with paper cut-outs and sticky tape where fixed masking was unavoidable.

Another medium Ciruelo would like to explore more in the future is oil painting. He loves it, but the snag with oils is the drying time – it is hopelessly slow for commissioned illustrations or even free works, for which his time is also limited. The attraction is that in oil painting the colours are mixed on the canvas, which is how Ciruelo feels it should be. Also the paint is opaque, unlike airbrush ink which allows the underlying colour (usually the whiteness of the artboard) to show through.

Speaking of colour, Ciruelo feels that perhaps the time has come to confess a little trade secret that he has kept from art directors for many years, seeing that he has probably done enough work for it to no longer matter. What is this, some technical secret? 'In a way,' he says. 'I am *daltónico.*' *Daltónico*? 'It means, more or less, colour blind. I cannot see shades.'

Reading Nature's Poem (1988)
A submission for a poster contest in Barcelona on the theme of children's books.

This is a bit like Pavarotti confessing to being tone deaf. Does he mean that all colours are just different shades of grey to him? Emotionally speaking yes, it seems. He can physically distinguish most colours but they mean nothing to him and he cannot imagine how Matisse and other Impressionists worked, almost completely abandoning form so they could play with colour. His own primary interest is in form and tone contrast, colour is something he has had to work at intellectually, compensating for his natural deficiency by reasoning and building up a catalogue of other people's reactions to colours and colour combinations. In his youth Ciruelo was forever asking his sister Lorena's advice on colour, now his wife Daniela bears the brunt of the questioning.

This difficulty with colour means that sculpture has always had a great attraction and is something else Ciruelo hopes to explore in the future. A current project reserved for when he finds the time is to make a dragon's skull, starting with one from the more humble cow which will be carved away in some places and built up in others with polyester.

Any other secrets he would care to reveal while the mood is upon him? Well, only perhaps that he always keeps a mirror nearby when working so the composition can be checked from a distance and defects shown up in the reversed image. Sometimes also he sketches on transparent acrylic sheets for similar reasons; but these are not great secrets as they are quite common practices among artists and illustrators.

Perhaps what might be more useful to know is something about Ciruelo's mental approach to his work. He likens it to a form of yoga, a discipline in which he is interested but feels no need to practise directly because he has his own Occidental version of it. As a youth he also took up the martial arts for a time – karate, tai kwon do and judo – and loved them not just for the physical training but their mental disciplines, their aim of bringing body and mind into harmony. Along with his other sporting interests they were dropped when he began work and no longer had time for such luxuries, but they taught many lessons which he finds still apply to life in general and work in particular.

Extracting useful lessons from what might to others seem dead episodes of the past is a recurring characteristic of Ciruelo's approach to life. He left piles of illustrations behind in Argentina for which he does not particularly want to be remembered, but he does still give them credit for having provided him with a masterly technique at an early age, plus the ability to work at lightning speed. It is a point of pride with him that he has never yet missed a deadline and usually manages to deliver early, unlike a certain illustrator friend of his in Madrid who on principle always leaves his commissions to the last possible moment.

English Sports (1989)
Illustration for an article in Spanish
Playboy. One of the first pictures
Ciruelo achieved by scraping a
painted surface.

Denim Can (1986)
An advert in Argentina.

Sony Tapes (1989)

Socks and Sneakers (1983)
An early work done at the age of eighteen mostly in ballpoint with washes of watercolour. The background was airbrushed in his own time with the equipment of the advertising agency where he worked. The shiny ball is a recent addition enabling the picture to be entered for a Christmas competition. It is removable, being painted on masking film.

Waterfall (1983)
Again the main instrument used was a ballpoint pen. The cost and scarcity of art materials in Argentina was a great stimulus for clever improvisation. Now in Spain, Ciruelo is still discovering materials and techniques which equivalent European illustrators take completely for granted. Which only goes to prove that in the end talent and perseverance count for more than the tools of the trade.

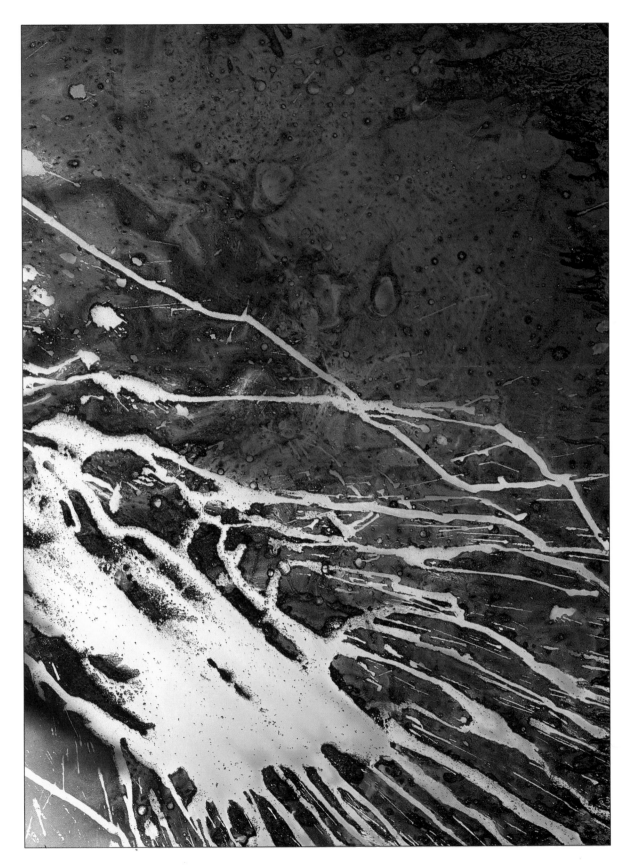

LEFT Jorge Flying in the Art Department (1984)
An early and favourite portrait of Ciruelo's brother, now an art
director in Buenos Aires. The main figure was drawn primarily in
ballpoint at the age of nineteen and has been retouched many
times since. The background is a recent addition.

Shapes (1984)
Jackson Pollock approach was adopted
here. Water was first thrown onto white
board so the marbling was repelled
from the wet areas.

Cities of the Dead (1990)
Cover illustration for a novel by Michael Paine.

The Embassy House (1989)
Cover illustration for a novel by
Nicholas Proffitt.

OVERLEAF **Masking Collage** (1989)
A collage made from discarded pieces of the masking film used in
airbrushing. Some are from illustrations in this book.

Bullseye (1987)
Video cover.

Cleanliness is a True Sign of Civilisation (1989)
Poster for a clean-up campaign in Ciruelo's current home town of Sitges (which is nearby Barcelona, capital of Catalonia). The language used in the poster is Catalan.

Warrior: Riposte (1990)
Book cover for the *Battletech* trilogy.

R<small>IGHT</small> **Cyclops** (1989)
Book cover.

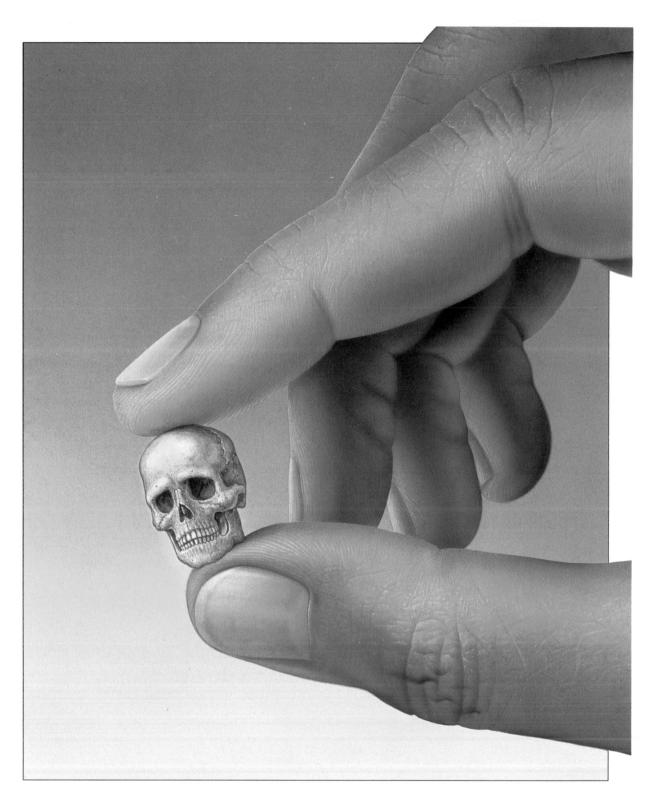

Miniature Skull (1986)
Originally used as an advert for an Argentine medical
laboratory with a pill in place of the skull.

Black Connection (1989)
Illustration for a *Playboy* article about drugs which mentioned
that a common way of passing them on is by kissing.

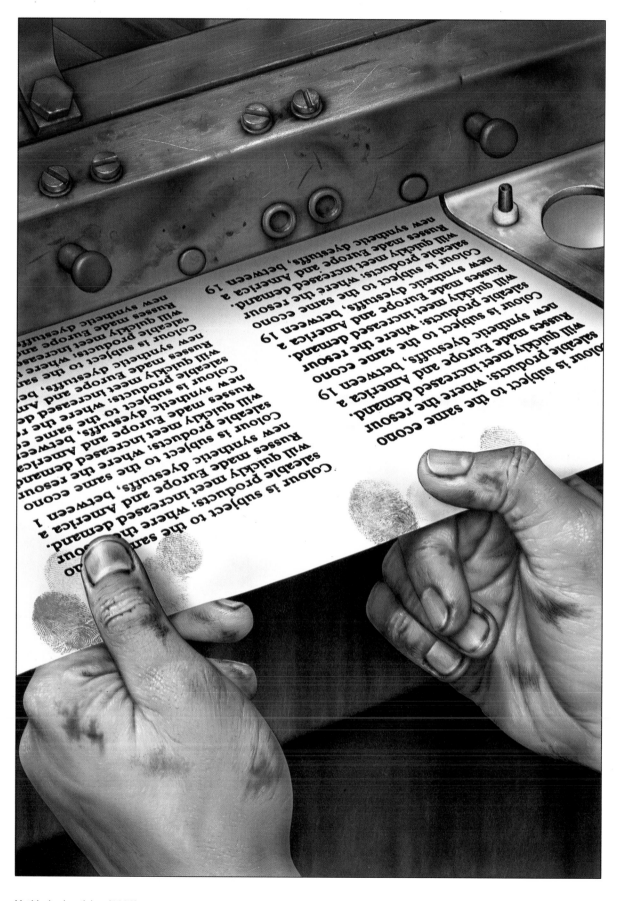

Untitled advertising (1989)

Untitled advertising (1989)

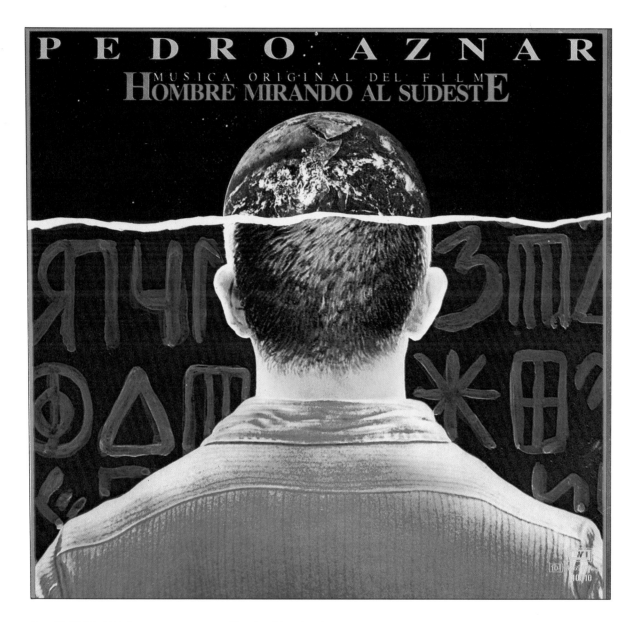

LEFT Rubbish (1989)
Another poster design for the clean-up campaign in Sitges.

Man Looking Southwest (1985)
Record cover for a film soundtrack. In fact the design was originally for a poster. Not realizing the film was going to become famous Ciruelo neglected to sign any contract for the work and so was paid nothing for this use of it. However, he loves Pedro Aznar's music so has no hard feelings about it.

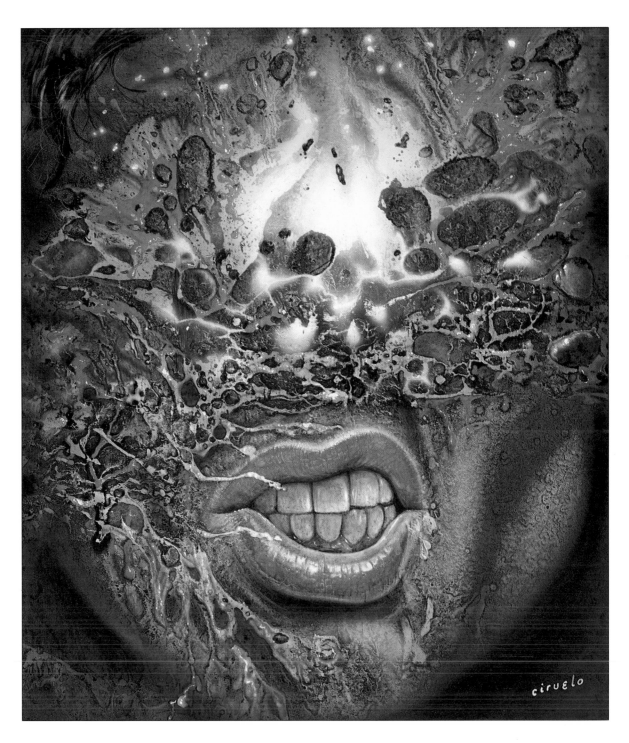

Personal Nuclear Explosion (1985)
Free work, the idea being suggested by a particularly lively piece of marbling. Later it appeared on the cover of an Argentine comic magazine.

RIGHT **The Legend of Huma** (1988)
Cover for a novel by Richard A. Knaack, part of the *Dragonlance* series whose Spanish logo is the work of Daniela Cabral.

OTHER DIMENSIONS

As a teenage Ciruelo, like many others, loved the gore of horror stories. His interest has waned since then but he can usually rise to the occasion when asked or when inspiration strikes.

Largely this is because many of the standard bugbears employed in the horror genre do not for him hold any terrors at all. Take insects for example. A common view of most insects is that their only saving grace is being small enough to squash easily, so tinkering with the laws governing their size and/or numbers has long been a favourite device of horror, fantasy and science fiction writers trying to stir up a bit of apprehension; but all insects have a certain beauty in Ciruelo's eye. In experiments he has sometimes combined insect and female bodies to try to bring out this beauty – he and his wife chase flies out of the window rather than swat them.

In this they do not go quite as far as their friend Oscar Chichoni in Italy who feeds flies on sugar and honey, but the principle is the same. To Ciruelo ants are as important as mammals and he will go to almost Tibetan lengths not to squash them. Likewise with salamanders. In the Middle Ages these creatures commanded a certain respect because it was believed they lived in fire, but nowadays most people find them at best fascinatingly ugly, at worst revolting. To Ciruelo, though, they are beautiful and he would love one as a pet.

With science fiction Ciruelo has similarly mixed feelings. That is to say, he does have a certain feel for the subject but hardly rates as a full-blooded enthusiast because, for reasons given earlier, wherever nature and technology are in conflict he is on nature's side.

However, where there is no conflict he is definitely interested in machines. In everyday life he has an instinct for how they work and how they can be improved. He has many ideas for improving airbrush design, for example, and is always tinkering with and modifying his bicycle, quite apart from inventing machines in his head to solve various problems he sees. He has mixed feelings about cars though, mainly because of the terrible traffic jams in Barcelona and the effect this has on the people condemned to endure them because of the lack of good public transport, himself and Daniela included.

In Ciruelo's view one of the greatest inventions in history was the humble wood screw – a symbol of practicality so perfect it is also beautiful. The way forward for science and technology, he believes, is shown by Roger Dean's futuristic buildings which aim to be completely integrated with the landscape, rather than defying it as is so often the case now.

Hell House (1988)
Book cover.

The Bones (1989)
Book cover. The scraping technique was again used here for
highlights and texture.

RIGHT **Minotaur** (1989)
Book cover.

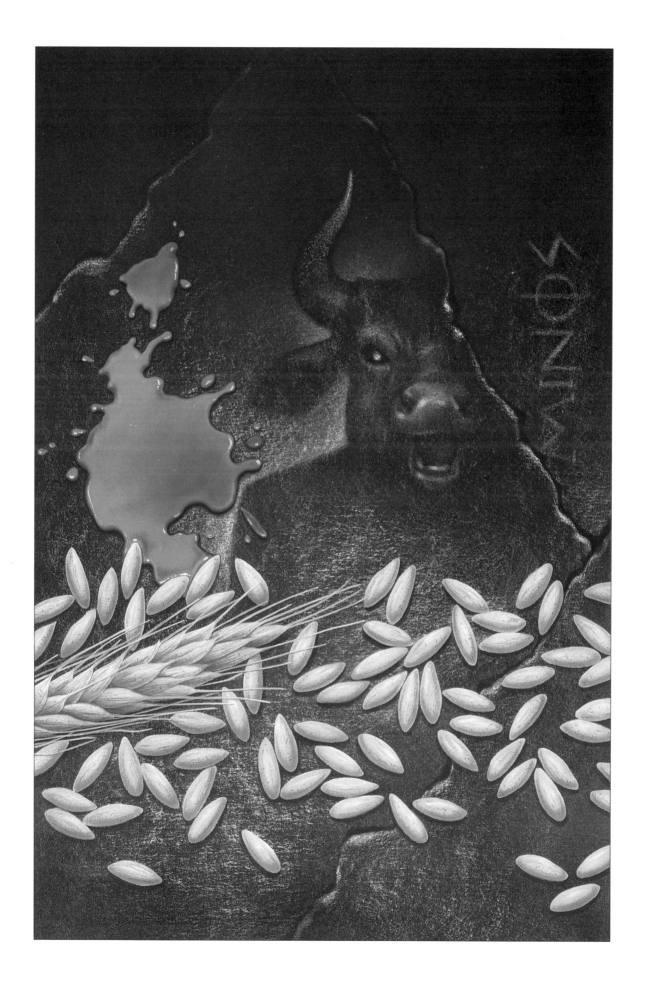

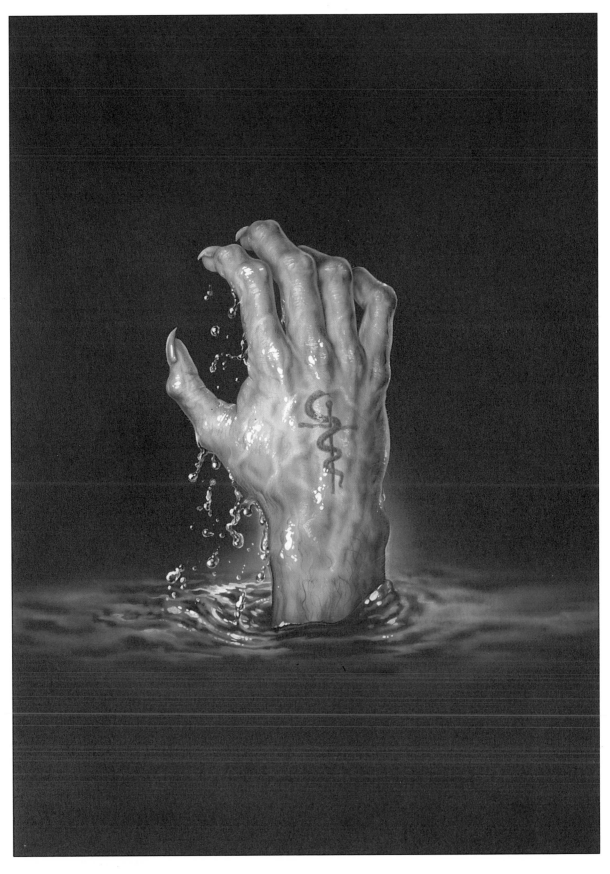

Deliver Us from Evil (1989)
Book cover. Definitely not the hand that raised Excalibur from the lake!

RIGHT **The Nameless** (1989)
Book cover.

Alien Syndrome (1988)
Computer game cover.

RIGHT **The Soldier** (1989)
Computer game cover.

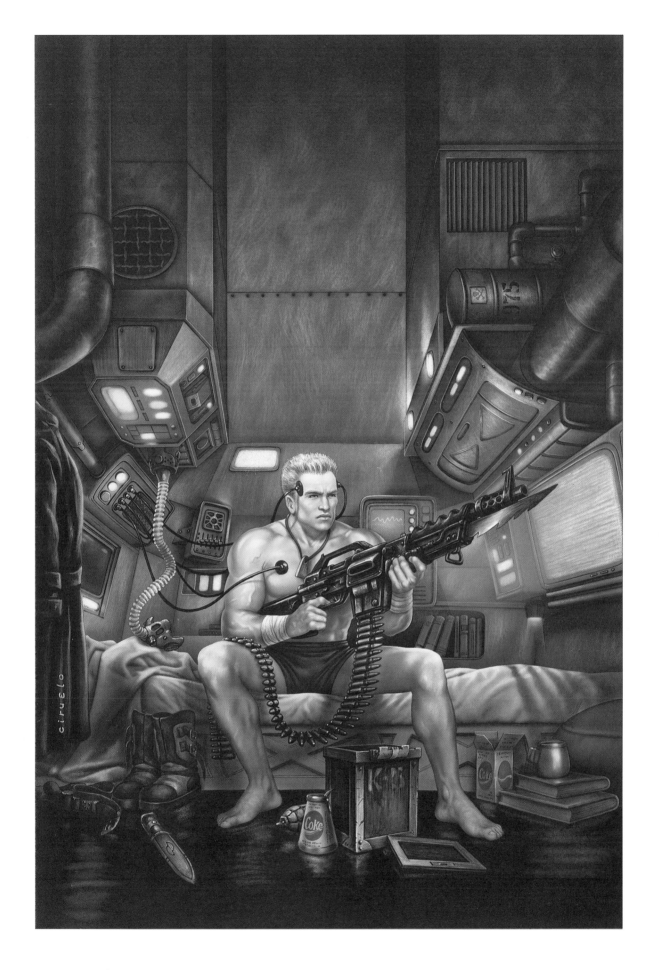

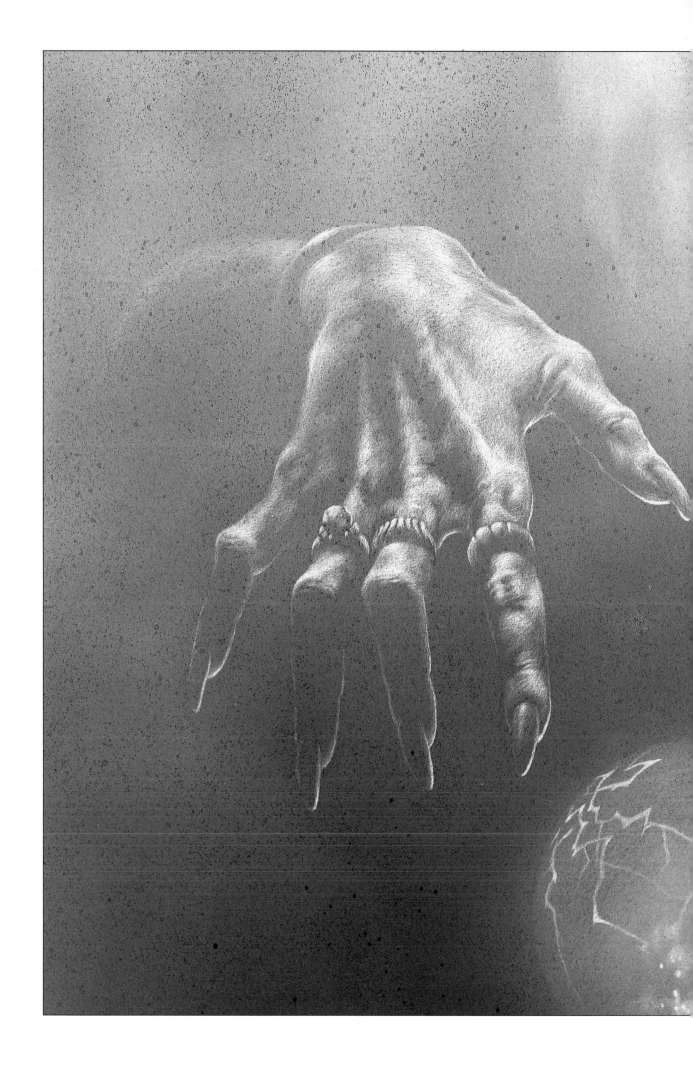

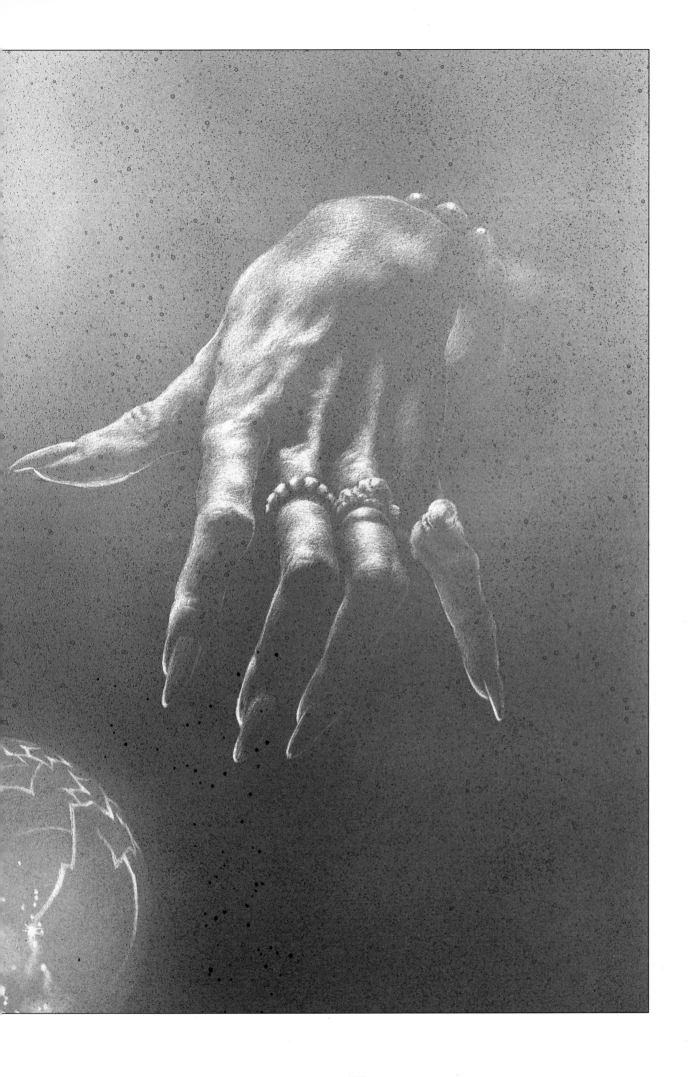

Dragon (1990)
The first of a series of about sixty illustrations for a collection of dragon legends proposed by Timun Mas, the Spanish publishing house for whom Ciruelo does most of his cover work. This is the project in whose favour his own brainchild Magma was shelved. The composition was dictated partly by the publishers' suggestion that it be used also on a bookmark, a useful way of getting paid twice for the same work.

RIGHT **Necroscope** (1990)
Book cover. The first of a set of six pictures using the scraping technique which is particularly effective, as here, in capturing the texture of bone.

PREVIOUS PAGES **Ghosts** (1990)
Illustration for a *Playboy* article on the occult. Achieved by scraping and working the highlights only.

TWENTIETH-CENTURY DREAMS

Here we are at the last chapter. What remains to be said? On one level, any number of things because how can one hope to do anything like a complete portrait of an artist in the space of a few thousand words? On another level, not much at all because the pile of notes beside me looks distinctly sparse. The text for this book arose from four days of interview in London in the week after Easter 1990. Correction, three and a half days. On the final day, when we arrived at the point of deciding what to talk about in the final chapter we realized, after a couple of hours of twiddling our thumbs and staring at the ceiling, that your interviewer had run out of questions and the interviewees (Ciruelo and Daniela) had run out of things they wanted to say. So we went for a wander round London instead. Which is in itself fairly remarkable because on the one side was an almost zero knowledge of Spanish and on the other a three month course in speaking English.

Would you like to know how London appeared to them? Why not? First of all, compared to Buenos Aires it is enormously green. Not just the parks which run through the centre of the city but all the gardens and the trees growing out of the pavements. In the parks they came across squirrels for the first time not only wild but feeding out of the hands of people, as were the rather scruffy sparrows and definitely more dapper ducks. Compared to Barcelona (which, before anyone is tempted to get smug about this, has traffic problems which place it in the world's top league) it is remarkably traffic-free and all the drivers astonishingly polite.

What else? The Tate Gallery managed to spring a few surprises. The Pre-Raphaelites met with perhaps the most approval as a general class; Richard Dadd's painting *The Fairy-Feller's Master Stroke* prompted wonder, admiration and finally the perfectly correct conclusion that he must have been mad, upon the discovery that the leaves not only looked perfectly life-like but their paint had been sculpted to match the original surface. Highest marks, though, went to the nineteenth-century painter John Martin. On being told of how Martin's vision of the end of the world had caused a riot on its first unveiling, with people fainting from vertigo and being torn between falling into the picture or simply to the floor, Ciruelo came to the conclusion that the power of illustrators to provoke such reactions had been undermined by *Star Wars* and the like.

However, this is I suppose rather by the way. There are as it happens quite a few items of information which I have not managed to fit in so far. There are other places where they could be squeezed in but if they had fitted there naturally they wouldn't

17th December 1989 (1989)
Free work, an experiment in contrasting not only textures but styles. The traces of realism in the foreground figures was achieved by scraping a dark painted surface and touching the result up with coloured pencils. Their likeness to Giacometti sculptures is accidental because Ciruelo has never to his knowledge come across them. The title commemorates the bloodshed in Bucharest which triggered the Romanian revolution.

now be left over. So, let us just take them as they come and forget about presenting the facts in any particular order.

For instance, no mention has been made so far of the fact that both Ciruelo's grandfathers are of Spanish extraction while both his grandmothers are Austrian. The former is not altogether surprising since Argentina used to be a Spanish colony. The latter is a bit, but only because their non-Spanish roots are the same. As in the United States, all kinds of Europeans have emigrated to Argentina over the years. In the south of the country one can discover whole communities which might have been transported *en masse* by magic from Germany, Wales or England, all speaking their own language and perpetuating the customs of their homelands (albeit on a different timescale).

Computer Car (1989)
Magazine cover.

RIGHT **Violet Car** (1988)
Part of a larger illustration which Ciruelo felt was spoiled by the main figure.

Party Action (1987)
Free work, a sample to tempt
publishers.

RIGHT **Meneses** (1985)
Early illustration for a comic magazine
cover in Argentina. As before, the main
character of Meneses, created by
Solano Lopez, is taken from the comic
and fleshed out.

Daniela Cabral is of Italian extraction so, as it happens, where they now live in Europe is a very reasonable compromise between their ancestral loyalties.

What else remains? Has anyone assumed that throughout the interviews we carefully skirted round the topic of a certain breakdown in good relations between our two countries in recent years? If so they are wrong because it arose as naturally as everything else. In raising the subject your interviewer had in mind the verdict of the Argentine sage Jorge Luis Borges that the Falklands–Malvinas war was like two bald men fighting over a comb. However, one needs to be both very old and very wise to get away with a comment like that, even if you do believe it will be the general opinion in a hundred years. What I did ask was whether Ciruelo had felt any conflict of loyalties during the trouble, seeing how it was the Englishman Roger Dean who first pointed the way forward, followed by several other more or less British illustrators? Or, come to that, did he not feel a little uneasy now because his book was about to be published first of all in London?

The reply I think would have pleased old Jorge: 'All artists are brothers whatever their nationality,' Ciruelo said. Hmmm. It's a bit tricky finding anything weighty enough to follow that. Perhaps we should call it a day here. Oh no, maybe not. What's this? A note from the editor: 'Dear Nigel, have you told them how old Ciruelo is yet?' Come to think of it, I don't think I have. All right then, if you must know, he is twenty-six years old at the time of writing. Which means that he was born in July 1963.

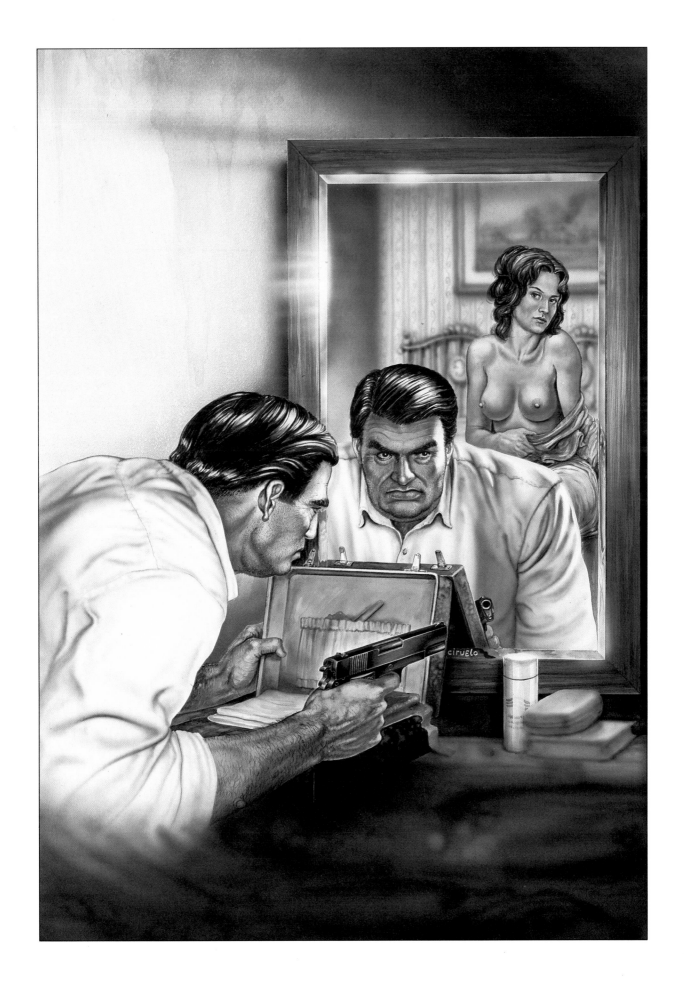

LEFT **Lightning Attack** (1985)
Free work.

Happy CD (1989)
Magazine cover.

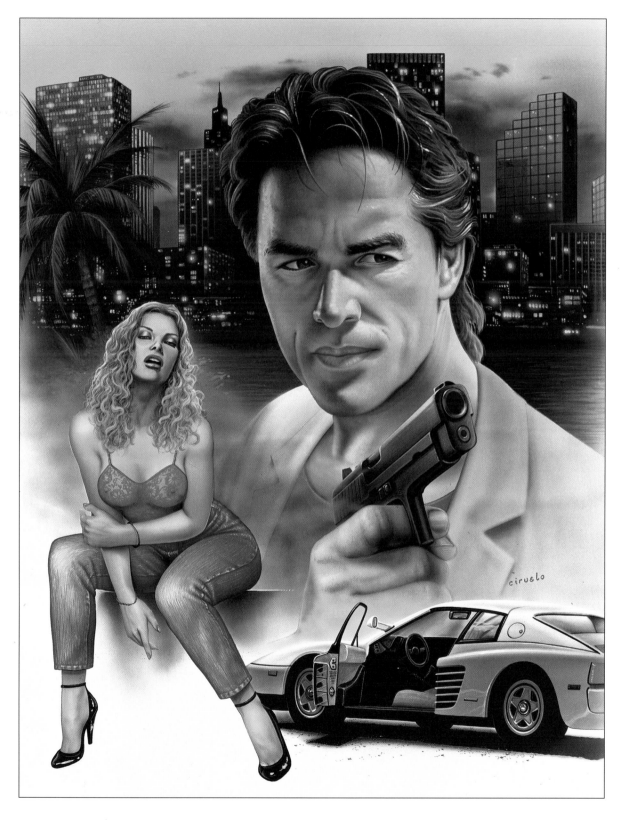

LEFT **Sex and Violence** (1988)
Cover for a comic magazine in Barcelona.

Miami (1988)
Book cover, one of a set of six featuring the same character.

Ciruelo Logo (1989)

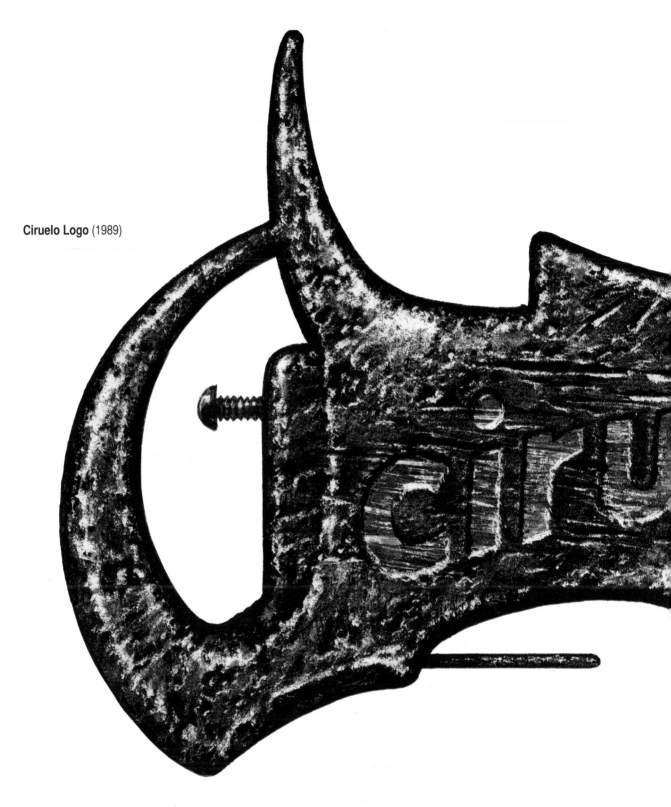

Forgotten Realms (1988)
Logo.

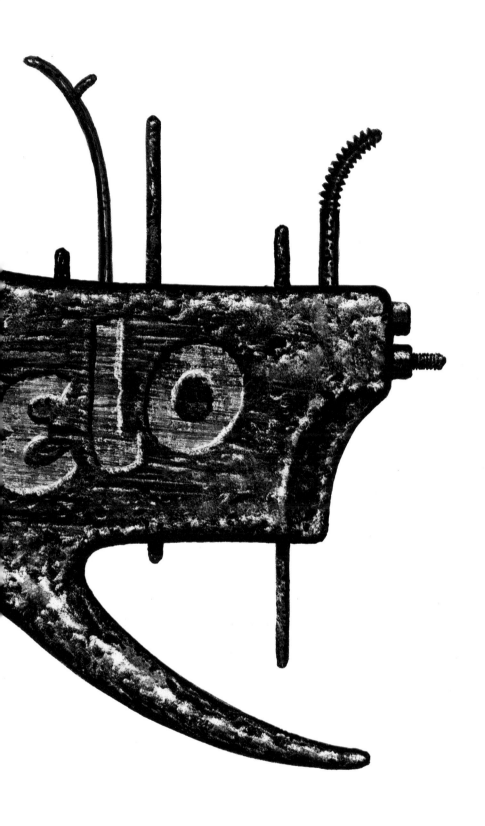

After the War (1989)
Logo.

Crazy for Trains (1989)
Illustration for a *Playboy* article using a new technique of
dipping pens and ink.

Black Cat (1987)
Free work.

LEFT Watering Technology (1989)
Computer magazine cover. When tackling these computer
pictures Ciruelo tried to inject a little humour into them
because he felt that most of such magazine covers were
serious almost to the point of boredom. The publishers took
some persuading that this was a good idea but he
occasionally won his case.

Cables (1983)
When humour was frowned upon the alternative was to do
something dramatic. The style adopted was clear and simple
to try and catch the eye while not interfering too much with
the title and other lettering.

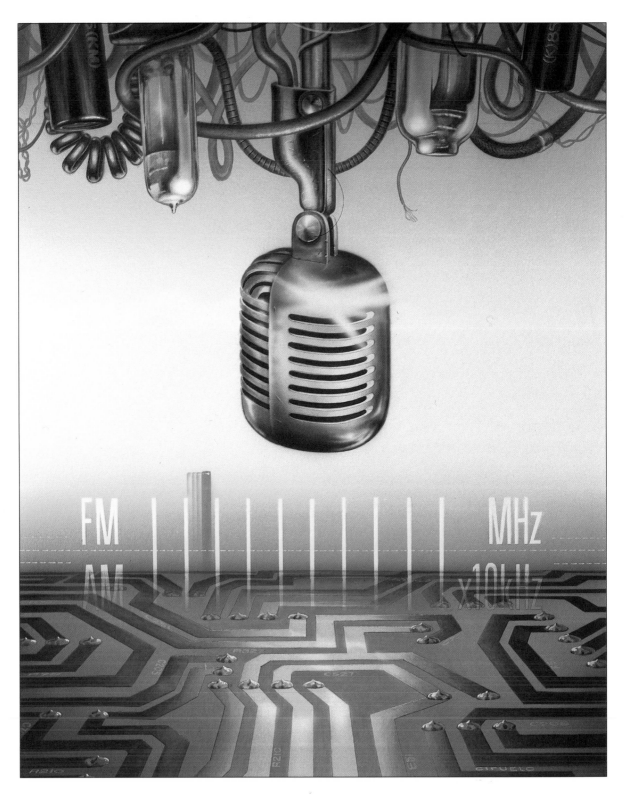

Radio Today and Yesterday (1988)
Illustration for a *Playboy* article about
old and new radio technology.

The Kruschev Objective (1988)
Cover for a book which was apparently based on a true incident involving Kruschev. At the publishers' request no figures were included in the scene and it so happens that the ploy is very effective in this case, arousing one's curiosity more probably than if we could see the preceding action.

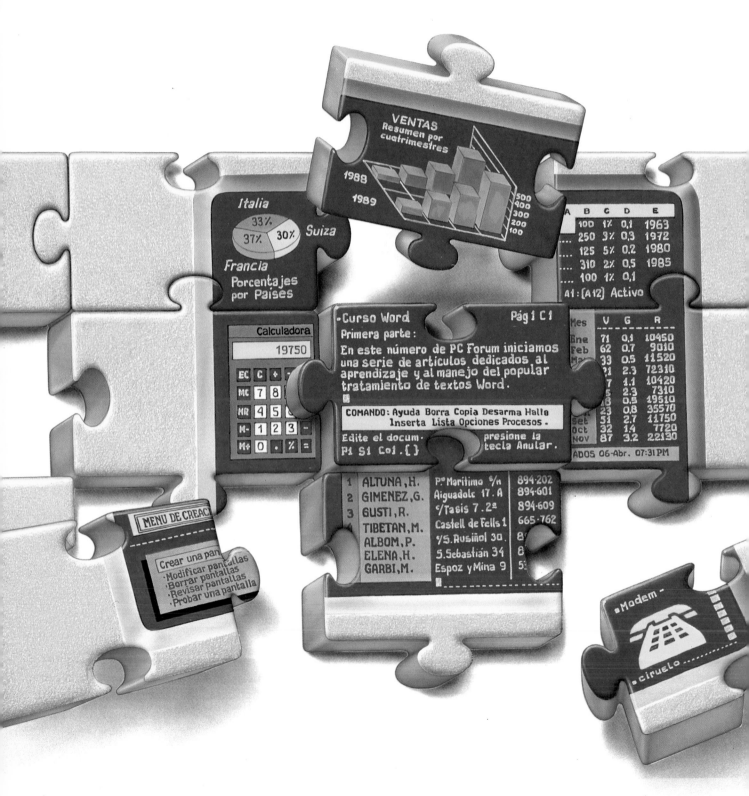

Puzzle (1989)
Magazine cover.

The Book (1989)
Magazine cover.

PC Superman (1989)
Magazine cover.

Army Knife (1989)
Magazine cover.

ACKNOWLEDGEMENTS

On leaving school Ciruelo sat three days of exams at an art college in Buenos Aires, and did very well, but in the end could not face the prospect of studying six years for a degree before he could start looking for a job. So his real teachers are the many illustrators mentioned in this book who have influenced his work, whom he would like to thank even though most were unaware of their contribution to his life. Of those he has met he would particularly like to thank Juan Giminez and Horacio Altuna for providing friendship as well as encouragement and advice.

Also he would like to thank Timun Mas publishing house for so many interesting commissions, Hubert Schaafsma for publishing this book, and Nigel Suckling for his work on the text. And most of all Ciruelo would like to dedicate his work to his mother.